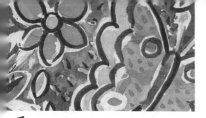

CW00689724

the LOVE story
by Lynn Green

CONTENTS

Cover design: Ross Advertising and Design Limited · Designer: Paul Edwards · Inside illustrations: Paulo Baigent · Typeset by HWTypesetters, Norwich · Printed by Ebenezer Baylis & Son Limited, The Trinity Press, Worcester and London · © Scripture Union 1994, 130 City Road, London EC1V 2NJ·ISBN 086201 816 1

The 'love generation' first captured the world's attention about 25 years ago. It began with a small, fringe group of radical young people with flowers in their hair. Their message of love fired the imagination of people everywhere and with remarkable speed they changed the vocabulary, fashion, music and general lifestyle of an entire generation.

Love was their message: they sang, talked and preached about it the world over. These flower people also succeeded in influencing the press, politicians and other leaders of society. And, in the process, the meaning of love was redefined.

Even though they used a familiar word, they were using it to mean things it had not meant before. For them, love meant that everyone was free to live for their own enjoyment. Their philosophy was often expressed in the simple statement: 'If it feels good, do it!' They promoted freedom from committed relationships – everyone, whether married or single, should be free to sleep with whoever they wished. Their beliefs included: never condemning anyone or any idea – because 'there is no right or wrong'; and granting everyone complete personal liberty to do *anything*, whatever that might be.

RESULTS

This experiment with a new kind of love has since been tried for a full generation. The flower people, now older and filling places of influence and power, have given birth to and raised another generation who are themselves reaching adulthood. Their philosophy of a new kind of love has permeated society at all levels and borne its fruit. So how does it taste?

Violent crime has risen ten-fold, or more. Divorce rates have sky-rocketed. Millions of babies have been aborted. Child abuse has become a major cause for concern. Pornography, and the so-called sex industry, has spread around the world, making billions in profits while destroying thousands of lives. At the same time, the world is experiencing an epidemic of sexually transmitted diseases.

This effort to change the meaning of love has demonstrated that the human race is not competent to be the final authority on such matters. Whenever we try to make changes which contradict what God has already said, the results are disastrous.

GOD IS LOVE

Jesus said that the greatest commandment is, 'Love the Lord your God with all of your heart and with all your soul and with all your mind and with all your strength.' The second is this: 'Love your neighbour as yourself' (Mark 12:30, 31). He was talking about a different kind of love from the one the Beatles had in mind when they released the anthem of the love generation, 'All you need is love'.

God has told us that *he* is love, so we must look to *his* nature and being for its true meaning. That can be best understood by reading the Bible and asking for the Holy Spirit's help.

LOVE FOR YOU

As you work through this booklet, alongside a *New International Version* (or any other modern translation) of the Bible, you will read and think about some of the scriptures through which

God makes his love known. When you see how much God's love has cost him and begin to understand more of how he wants you to love him and others, then the true meaning of real love will become clearer.

But the purposes of these readings go much deeper. The reading of the Bible is never meant to be just a mental exercise. Through the scriptures, the Holy Spirit works for change in us so that we might be more like Jesus.

Since this is God's loving purpose, it is best to make it our purpose too. We can do this by starting each day's time with God with a prayer, asking him to speak as we think about what we are reading. But, remember, God speaks to those who are willing to do what he says, so it is important always to read the Bible with a readiness to make the necessary changes in our lives.

GETTING THE MOST OUT OF IT

We will be looking at *The Love Story* from four angles. Each section's Bible readings challenges us to apply what we read to our daily living if we want to grow with Jesus. Some things asked of us might sound, and be, very difficult. But, remember, the greatest spiritual growth comes when we have attempted difficult things, worked at them and succeeded in obedience to God.

You will be more likely to benefit from these Bible readings if, when you think God has spoken about something in particular, you write it down. It might be a good idea to put that piece of paper in this booklet, or some other place where you will be sure to read it again soon. However you choose to remind yourself, just be sure to review regularly those things which God has brought to your attention.

As you allow the Holy Spirit to change you by the power of his love, it will soon become noticeable in your relationships with others. But you may need some help in working through the implications of what God is saying to you, so if you know of any mature Christians who can help you grow through these readings, do plan to spend some time sharing with them. Perhaps you could ask them for a reminder now and then about obeying the things God has said to you.

As you learn about the meaning of love, ask God to transform you more and more so that you become firmly convinced of his love for you, more committed in your love for him and more empowered to love others.

the
love
story

Growing for Jesus means being sure of God's love and letting those around us know that we love him. Our first section sets out to ground and strengthen our faith, to free us of any feelings of being unloved and unlovable.

God loves me

Several years ago, I received an invitation to speak at a discipleship training week in South Africa. That invitation provided me with a most unusual and enjoyable opportunity because my father was also invited. Together, we were asked to share the teaching ministry on the subject of 'The Fatherhood of God'.

About 150 young people were present that week and listened eagerly to the teaching sessions which my Dad and I gave. It was encouraging to experience God using our ministry to open up important issues for so many of them.

In the counselling sessions between lectures, we had the joy of seeing several young people set free from hurt and bitterness. Many were, for the first time, beginning genuinely to believe that God loved them.

While all these aspects of the week were exciting, there was another ingredient which was even more enjoyable: the occasion and its subject gave me the opportunity to understand how deeply God had blessed *me* personally through my own father. Both publicly and in private conversations, I was able to express my love and appreciation for him. Added to that, I discovered more about how he had developed into such a good parent, in spite of his very difficult early home life.

LESSONS THROUGH PAIN

At the time of my father's early childhood, his father had been a successful farmer in midwest USA. Then the great drought of the 1930s struck and my grandfather lost everything. More than thirty years later, he became a committed Christian in the last weeks of his life, but the intervening years had been spent in bitterness and anger. Although the members of his family often felt the brunt of that anger, my own father didn't go on to be harsh or unkind towards us, his children.

In South Africa, Dad explained how he had made a commitment to Christ in his early teens. Though young, with little Christian maturity, he knew that his experiences could either lead to bitterness or learning opportunities in his own life. He was determined to forgive his father and do his best to learn from the injustices he had suffered.

As a result of this wise decision and with God's help, he was to develop into a strong, loving adult with few scars from the past.

During that time in South Africa, I developed a new gratitude for the love my parents had shown me. And, because I had never been given any cause to doubt their love, when I was first told that God my heavenly Father loved me it wasn't too difficult to comprehend.

That week brought home to me in a real way what great blessing I had received by God's grace through my parents. It was *their* love that had prepared me to receive *God's* love. My appreciation of that blessing grew

the
love
story

even more as we spoke with those who came forward for counselling.

I recall one confused, hurting girl who had been the victim of abuse from her father. To her way of thinking and feeling, the fact that God was her father was certainly *not* good news. 'Father' had become a word which made her cringe.

She couldn't believe God (*or anyone else*) could really love *her*. Several long sessions gave her much-needed confidence and time to uncover the pain and confusion she had experienced. And, as we prayed for her, she began to understand God's pure, strong, trustworthy love. It was a changed person that went home at the end of the week, even though she still had many issues to work through.

FOUNDATIONS OF LOVE

Everyone is born with a need to be loved – God designed it that way. He also created and placed us in a family environment where love can be expressed. From the earliest stages, our lives are meant to be shaped mostly by two parents who care for us. That parental love, at best, is a dim reflection of God's amazing love for his children. And it's meant to lay foundations on which the love of God can build as we grow older. If those foundations are secure, then it will not be difficult to believe in God's love for us. However, if they are faulty, we may experience great difficulty in receiving it. But we can be sure he won't give up on us; his love is sufficient to overcome any deficiencies in our lives.

The Bible readings covered in our first section bring home to us this amazing love. Some of us find it easy to accept, while others perhaps believe it in their mind, but find their heart will not agree.

Whether you find it easy or difficult, make no mistake, the reality of God's love is firm. That love was demon-

strated for you and me through the life of Jesus. It is explained and emphasised again and again throughout the New Testament. But, without the ministry of the Holy Spirit, even the most striking passages of scripture are no more than words on paper.

If we really long to know the love of God personally, then we need the revealing power of the Holy Spirit to understand it. Even if our family background is one where we have been secure in the love of others, we still need to ask God for a revelation of his love. If, on the other hand, we find it difficult to receive love, then our need for such a revelation is all the more necessary.

WHERE TO START

Before you begin to read the Bible on this wonderful subject of love, stop and pray. Ask God to open up your heart to his love and welcome his Spirit into your life. Ask him to strengthen the bonds of love between you, so you can rest secure in the knowledge that you are personally and deeply loved by God himself. Return to this prayer again and again, and finish each daily session with a time of meditation and prayer.

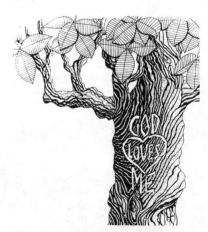

God loves me

Day 1
PROOF POSITIVE
John 4:9,10; 3:16, 17

The Apostle John was known as 'the disciple whom Jesus loved' because he was particularly close to Jesus. In the gospel which he wrote and in his letters to believers, he majored on the importance of a love relationship, first with God and then with others.

The cornerstone of John's message, made very clear in today's Bible verses, is that God has an *extraordinary* love for us. It was because of this love, he became a man and died on our behalf. Spend some time thinking about his love, a love so strong that he was willing to make this ultimate sacrifice even though no one loved him first.

Although we may sometimes feel totally worthless and unlovable, God has set out to convince us that he really *does* love us. It seems that our own experience with life and personal guilt feelings can lead us to expect harsh treatment from God. Of course, this is what we deserve, but God is not a stern heavenly Father who seeks to condemn: his goal is to save. We may be prone to doubt the love of God at times, but the fact remains that God himself became a man and then died on *our* behalf. Surely, this is proof positive that his love is big enough to encompass *everyone*, regardless of what we have done or how unworthy we feel.

Prayer starter:
Thank you, Lord, for all the proof you have given of your love for me, especially...

Day 2
FRIENDSHIP RESTORED
Romans 5:6-11

God has taken the initiative towards us. Everyone on earth has been, and is, in exactly the same position, regardless of how good or bad they appear to be: we have all been separated from God with no love for him and no power or desire to overcome our separation.

But we can thank God for his rescue plan. Because of his overwhelming love, we have been justified before God. Everyone who has turned away from wrong and believes in Jesus stands guilt-free in God's eyes.

Even so, there is still more to our salvation. When Paul says we have received reconciliation, he is pointing out that all barriers between us and God have been removed so that we can enjoy friendship with our Creator.

God first created human beings for friendship with himself and with one another. In the *Genesis* account of creation we see God walking and talking with Adam and Eve every evening. Now there is nothing to keep us from enjoying fellowship with God again - we *are* reconciled. What an incredible commitment of love God has shown toward us! No wonder Paul says, 'we also rejoice in God through our Lord Jesus Christ' (v 11).

Are you taking advantage of this priceless opportunity for fellowship with our Father God?

Prayer starter:
Think about this as you come to him in prayer.

the
love
story

Day 3
IT LASTS FOREVER
Romans 8:28-39

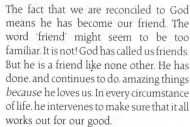

the
love
story

The fact that we are reconciled to God means he has become our friend. The word 'friend' might seem to be too familiar. It is not! God has called us friends. But he is a friend like none other. He has done, and continues to do, amazing things *because* he loves us. In every circumstance of life, he intervenes to make sure that it all works out for our good.

There is a persistent notion that the God who created the world set everything in motion and then left it to run according to the 'law of cause and effect'. But throughout the Bible, God is revealed as one who intervenes in human history. Even so, he's not only active in the most important aspects of history, his caring intervention also extends into the smallest details of our lives for our good.

And what is our good? – That we should become more and more like Jesus. Since Christ-likeness is God's best plan for us, not everything will go smoothly. Hebrews 5:8 points out that even Jesus 'learned obedience from what he suffered'. However, God assures us that he will never desert us – he will *always* keep us in his love. A love that is so strong and personal that no circumstance, no hardship, no demonic opposition can tear us away from our heavenly Father's tenacious care.

Verses to learn:
Commit to memory verses 38 and 39 before you pray.

Day 4
LOVED AS CHILDREN
Galatians 3:26-4:7

Our friendship with God is a remarkable demonstration of love and kindness, but it's more than this... We are loved as his own children. We are adopted into his family by the power of his Holy Spirit. This means that he is at work within our lives, helping us become more like Jesus. It also means that our Father God loves us with the same love he has for Jesus, and that certainly is the strongest love the world has ever known.

His Spirit within us has also changed the way we relate back to Father God. Instead of knowing him as the law-maker and judge, he gives us an urge to know him intimately – in the same way a child loves his or her father. The Greek word, *Abba* (v 6) best translates as 'Daddy' or 'Dad'. Its use here demonstrates that God extends a love and grace towards us which far exceeds anything we feel worthy of, even on our best days. Yet there is something God expects in return. He wants *us* to love *him*. God has taken the initiative, for we could never hope to earn what is freely offered to us. All we can do is *accept* our adoption with love and worship for our 'Abba'.

Prayer starter:
Father, I worship and adore you. You are worthy of so much praise. Forgive me for the times when I forget to worship you.

God loves me

Day 5
LOVE BEYOND DESCRIPTION
Ephesians 1:5-8

In an effort to describe God's love for us, Paul pushes his language to its limits. Using such words as 'lavish', 'glorious grace' and 'all wisdom and understanding', he gives the impression that we are loved to a degree which far exceeds our ability to understand fully or describe.

It is not unusual for Christians to understand God's love for them in the light of their own experience with human love. Yet, because human love can fail, disappoint and leave lasting scars, some believers are afraid to fully entrust themselves into anyone's hands – including God's. However, *his* love is entirely different from any other love we might have experienced. The love of God is something we can always depend on.

It is important to hold on to the fact that he adopted us as his children because he wanted to (v 5). God is under no obligation to love you or me. He does not love because it is his duty. It actually gives him great pleasure to have us as his children. When we come to him in prayer, our requests are not heard grudgingly. He is *delighted* to hear and answer us.

For action:
Set aside some time today just to thank God for the depth of his love for you. Remember, his love, which we sometimes tend to take for granted, is the most important commitment that will ever be made to us.

Day 6
GIVES LIFE ETERNAL
Ephesians 2:1-10

Understanding more about God's love is easier when we realise what he has saved us from. As sinners, pursuing our own desires, we were playing into the hands of Satan whose goal it is to destroy. Seeking to please ourselves, we were slowly being led into a bondage which would last for eternity.

The more people try to achieve independence and personal pleasure, the more they are held captive by the 'ruler of the kingdom of the air', (Ephesians 2:2). We can never thank God enough for setting us free from Satan's captivity.

However, that is only *part* of the amazing story. We take in more of what God's love means to us when we understand something of his plans for our future.

The salvation we experience now is just the beginning of a perfect life which will last ' forever. For now, we have only a glimpse of what will be. We know we will reign with him (2 Timothy 2:12) and that we will be with Jesus in our heavenly Father's house (John 14:1-4). But, most of all, we know that God's plans for our future far exceed our most hopeful imaginations. 'No eye has seen, no ear has heard, no mind has conceived what God has prepared for those who love him' (1 Corinthians 2:9).

Prayer starter:
Ask God to give you assurance about the future and to show you what you should be doing for him now.

the
love
story

I know for certain!

Well, it's certainly been 'back to basics'! We've found out that for us to live a reasonably mature Christian life, we *must* be able to accept totally that God loves us.

PERSONAL! Let's be more personal for a moment: God wants *you* to accept fully in your mind, heart and emotions that he loves *you* with a love which will never let you down. If you still feel unable to trust his love, or need more convincing, then this is a good time to ask God to deal with you.

HELP! If you sometimes find it hard to believe that God loves you, I would like to suggest a prayer for you to use. You might be more comfortable with your own words, but here's something to get you started:

Father God, I know that you love me because the Bible makes it clear. But there are times when I find that hard to believe, so I ask for your help to experience more of your love in my life. I want to have a 'heart-knowledge' of your love, not just a 'head-knowledge'. Thank you for loving me.

extra

Day 7
LOVE WE CAN DEPEND ON
Hebrews 6:13-20

Everyone has a basic need for security, to find something or someone s/he can rely on without fear of being let down. The search to satisfy this need is pursued through many avenues: family love, relationships, money, positions of importance, houses, reputation. Yet our experience of life leads us to conclude that none of these things provide complete security – they can all fail.

This need for security is actually a void which stems from our separation from God. It is a longing for a relationship with him. And, while it might be temporarily appeased by other things, it cannot be fully satisfied by anything else.

To make his people secure in his love, God established his relationship with Abraham and his offspring by means of a formal agreement initiated by a solemn ceremony (Genesis 15). But God's new covenant is even more secure – he established it through the sacrifice of his own son. When Jesus died, he initiated a loving agreement in which we can find rock-solid security. He demonstrated that his love for us is great enough for him to be willing to pay the ultimate price. When our insecurities prompt us to question, 'Does he still love me?', the answer is a confident, 'Yes, I know he does because he died for me!'

For action:
Tell someone about your experience of the love of Jesus.

God loves me

Paying the price

Love can be costly and painful. Sometimes we bring the pain on our-selves; at other times, suffering comes through no fault of our own. Through no fault of *his* own, Jesus paid the price of making God's love known to us.

P:

Scandals involving Christian leaders are something we all hear about from time to time. But did you hear about the prophet who ended up marrying a prostitute? The remarkable thing is that he claimed God had led him to marry the woman - and, in the end, it seemed that he was right.

x

the love story

The prophet's name was Hosea. His whole life illustrated how God feels about the unfaithfulness of mankind. In the book of *Hosea* we read about a man who, at God's bidding, married an unfaithful and disreputable woman. She left him repeatedly; had children by other men, and even sold herself into prostitution. But while all this was happening her husband, Hosea, continued to love her. Every time she left home, he searched until he found her. He even paid a price to buy her back from a life of prostitution.

Through Hosea's heartache and disappointment, God demonstrates the depth of his love for all people. We can be sure he will go to any length to convince us of his love.

A love so great that it actually led to the death of his son, Jesus.

PAID IN FULL

The most familiar story in human history is probably the crucifixion of Jesus Christ. It's one we have all heard again and again. As a result, there is a tendency for us to miss some of its impact - *the wonder* - of this greatest of all love stories. Before you begin to read the account of Jesus' death on the cross, stop to think about the depth of love it portrays.

Jesus' death was the culmination of God's efforts over many generations to reach rebellious humankind. He had created the human race in his image so that we could enjoy a loving relationship with him and with one another. When we rebelled against him, he remained committed in his love for us. He didn't destroy his human creation, even though he could easily have done so.

Instead of exercising his unlimited power in a final act of judgement, God set out to win us back with his love. On the face of it, this seems an unusual way for God, who is all-powerful, to behave towards the people he created. Have you ever wondered why he didn't simply *make* people love him? And wouldn't it be possible for God to introduce one or two 'adjustments' so that we would always obey him?

The simple answer is, yes. God is powerful enough to change us into a 'clockwork' species, but such creatures would be incapable of freely loving God, or anyone else.

Think about it: a large part of why love means so much to us is the fact that someone has *chosen* to love us, even though they did not have to. Perhaps that's why God seeks to persuade us rather than just forcing us to do his will.

x

ying the price

IT'S BEEN SAID

God began his pursuit of the human race by sending messengers (*prophets*): men and women who spoke God's words and revealed more of his loving nature to people. One such prophet was Abraham: It was through him that God promised to create a nation to be an example of his covenant love. He told Abraham, and the generations of Jews who were his descendants, that, if they in turn would love him and serve him, he would bless them and demonstrate his love through them. (*See* Psalm 67 *as an example.*)

But that chosen nation refused consistently to respond to his love. And so God sent other prophets, warning them to turn from their rebellion and live a life of obedience to God's commands or else suffer the consequences. The nation of Israel took no notice of God's messengers. Instead, they killed or persecuted God's servants and further rebelled against his love by worshipping other Gods. The parable of the tenant farmers (Luke 20:9-18; *our first reading in the next series*), summarises how God responded to this ongoing rebellion. He didn't give up. He didn't destroy the nation, but continued to use all manner of means to persuade them to love and serve him.

EXPRESSION OF LOVE

As the prophets predicted, Jesus was born, and lived his life as a perfect expression of the love of God. Everywhere he went, he healed people, he delivered others from demons and set many free from their sins. His message was much more than words - he was the embodiment and ultimate illustration of love.

The people of Israel, excited about his miracles, flocked to see Jesus. But, as soon as he explained some of the demands of love, most of them deserted him (John 6:25-70). They didn't like the idea of a love which placed demands on *them.*

Though we are the ones who deserve to suffer death for our rebellion and sin, Jesus took it upon himself to suffer that punishment on our behalf. While we may claim to be grateful for the costly love which God has extended towards us, we must watch that we aren't deceiving ourselves. God's love makes demands upon us *now* just as surely as Jesus made demands on his hearers. Yet we too, may want to turn away from responding fully to the cost of love.

As you read of the death of Jesus, pray that your heart will be softened by the love of God, and ask that you might be among the few who love him wholeheartedly.

the
love
story

13

Day 8
IT COST GOD HIS SON
Luke 20:9-19

the
love
story

The crucifixion was no accident. Jesus was quite clear that he had come to give his life as a sacrifice for sin. When he told this parable, he revealed that he knew the leaders of the day would reject and, in due course, kill him. But that didn't deter him from his mission.

Long before Jesus became God in the flesh, God had counted the cost of redeeming humanity from their sin and lostness. He had already decided *who* would pay the ultimate price and thereby offer freedom to all who would take it. This is a depth of love we would know nothing about without God's clear demonstration. Jesus shows that God's love goes far beyond any other. Though we all have a God-given ability to love, we normally only love those who return our love in some way. But Jesus has loved, and still loves, those who reject him repeatedly.

The Bible and other records of history reveal how generation after generation has consistently conveyed one message to God: 'Leave us alone, we don't want to know!' Yet still God has persisted in his love and willingness to redeem all who will turn to him. In the light of such a persistent and costly love, how can we help but love him in return?

Prayer starter:
Father, I pray for... who refuses to listen when I talk about Jesus. Please break through with your love.

Day 9
OPPOSITION AND BETRAYAL
Luke 22:1-6

Is there anything that hurts more than betrayal by a close friend? The cross and the events which led to it brought deep tests to the Lord Jesus and the treachery of Judas must have been one of the most painful. Remember, Judas was a full member of the privileged inner ring of twelve disciples, and he lived in that circle of close friendships for three years. During that time, there is no evidence of him being a deceiver or betrayer. Though we cannot be sure of what motivated Judas, the text suggests that he had become greedy and then unbelieving. There are at least *two* vital lessons here:

● We must watch out for temptations such as greed. The fact that Judas fell away, should make us very careful. Paul says: 'So, if you think you are standing firm, be careful that you don't fall!' (1 Corinthians 10:12)

● Remember Jesus knows all about betrayal. No one will ever be *more* betrayed than he was. Yet he didn't become vengeful or bitter. He is always with us, ready to help us be forgiving as he was. No matter how badly we have been treated, Jesus shows us that we should – and can – forgive.

For meditation:
Take a close look at Matthew 6:14, 15.

Paying the price

Day 10
'MY BODY, MY BLOOD'
Luke 22:7-23

The Passover meal was celebrated each year by the Jews in remembrance of how God had delivered them from Egypt (Exodus 12:1-42).

At this last meal with his friends, Jesus showed that the Passover was not just a meal of remembrance, it was also a prophecy of a new covenant which he was poised to initiate.

Today, we are all very familiar with the account of the crucifixion, the day when God showed just how much he loves us. But on that last evening together, the disciples still did not understand what Jesus was doing. It had been a great challenge to their faith for them to believe fully that Jesus of Nazareth was in fact God in the flesh. Now could they *also* believe that his death would not be the end but lead on to his resurrection and save them (*and us*) from their sins?

Prayer starter:
Whenever we read this story, we should ask ourselves, do we still have a sense of wonder and awe? Or have we allowed its familiarity to deaden our responses?
Pray that God will restore within you the wondrous amazement that God could love you enough to die for you.

Day 11
STEADFAST DETERMINATION
Luke 22:39-53

If you knew the police would arrest you if you went to a certain place, would you go? Jesus knew that Judas had decided to help the officials apprehend him, yet he still went to his customary place on the Mount of Olives. It would not have been difficult for Jesus to have eluded his enemies that night, but he was determined to finish his difficult task.

Though he knew his time had come, the emotional demands of the ordeal awaiting him stretched his human abilities beyond their limit. Even so he dug deep and found supernatural strength – in the form of an angel. When Jesus had re-stated his determination to do the will of the Father, the resources of heaven, came to strengthen him.

The disciples were tested beyond *their* breaking point. They slept while Jesus prayed, and didn't realise they needed strength from heaven.

Tests come to everyone, and some of those tests are of such intensity that they can push us beyond our ability to endure. But just as Jesus was faithful in prayer for his disciples *then*, he is interceding *now* for each one of us (Hebrews 7:25). By the grace which is made available through his intercession, we can stand in the most difficult circumstances.

Prayer starter:
Pray for someone you know who is facing seemingly impossible circumstances.

the
love
story

Day 12
PHYSICAL AND VERBAL ABUSE
Luke 22:63-23:5

Have you ever been mocked, or accused of something you didn't do? Few things are more painful.

Jesus was laying down his life for sinful humanity. It would have been fitting if he had been surrounded by people who loved and worshipped him for what he was doing. Instead, he was experiencing some of the most despicable treatment we could ever imagine.

Keep in mind that Jesus was fully human and so experienced the same kind of emotions we experience. As the soldiers taunted and beat him, and then the religious leaders falsely accused him, he must have battled with a crushing sense of injustice. He had given himself to them in love and service. He had taught them, healed them and ministered to their needs – yet this was how they repaid him!

It is very hard to love those who reject us. When the pain of rejection is felt we usually react with anger or withdrawal. But Jesus kept right on loving.

If he was able to love those who caused him such pain, we can be sure that he keeps right on loving us when we fail him or stray from his love. He could immediately have called down heavenly retribution on his torturers, but he didn't. And the love he demonstrated then is also there for us.

Prayer starter:
Father, I pray for... who has hurt me deeply. I need your power to help me forgive.

Day 13
DEATH SENTENCE
Luke 23:6-25

In a sense, the sentence had been passed against Jesus long before Pilate or Herod saw him. In Revelation 13:8, John writes about the '... Lamb that was slain from the creation of the world.' God, in his love, had already considered the fate of the sinful human race and had put together his plan of salvation.

It remained for someone to call for Jesus' death. Who would it be? The manoeuvring of Pilate and Herod indicates no real desire to end his life. Both seemed to find him fascinating and disturbing, but not worthy of death. The religious leaders, on the other hand, thought differently. They would have put Jesus to death themselves, but didn't have the necessary authority. For this, they needed co-operation from the civil authorities, which they secured by using the crowds to pressurise Pilate.

These chief priests and rulers demonstrate the great danger of religious convictions mixed with arrogance and self-righteousness. It should provoke us to walk humbly, with an awareness of our own weaknesses – lest we also be found in unwitting opposition to God.

Check it out:
Read Isaiah 53 before you pray.

Paying the price

Day 14
IT'S A GIFT
Luke 23:26-49

Jesus gave his life – no one took it from him. Even though he was tried by the authorities, condemned to death and then led away to be executed, they didn't take his life – he gave it freely.

If Jesus had been executed by the Jews, he would not have been able consciously to bear the sins of humanity, because the Jews executed criminals by stoning and a victim of stoning normally died within a few minutes at most. Instead, he died at the hands of the Roman authorities who occupied Israel during his life. They had devised crucifixion as a method of execution which would strengthen their authority throughout the empire. It was a method which resulted in a slow, lingering death that could take days.

Jesus *willingly* submitted himself to die in this way, as it would leave him fully conscious over a period of hours. Then, while hanging there in agony, he suffered separation from his father as he paid the penalty for our sin. It was this weight of sin, and the consequent separation from his father, that took his life.

For meditation and prayer:
How, or why, would anyone freely submit to such agony? The only answer is love, the greatest love ever known – the love of God our Saviour who refused to abandon us to the punishment we deserve.

I can do it!

After reading and thinking about *why* Jesus died for us, we should be able to reach at least *two* firm conclusions:

- we are loved and...
- we should be able to love others, even though they may be hard to love.

ASSURANCE Already we have seen how the Bible emphasises God's love for us, but the assurance of that love can always go deeper.

Take some time now to thank God for his love for you. Remember, it is so strong that Jesus was willing to die for you.

EXAMPLE Think about how Jesus expressed love to the people around him even when they were betraying and finally killing him. In the light of his example, are there any valid excuses we can make for not loving someone? No way! – for no one has ever been treated worse than Jesus, yet *he* continued to love.

If there are people you find hard to love, ask for God's help to love them with an unconditional love. That is the kind of love Jesus has for us, and it's the kind of love he can help us to have for others.

War always brings its fair share of heroes: those who are willing to die for what they believe in and for the good of others. Our battle against the devil calls for the same unselfish love. We must take up our cross daily and follow Jesus.

ve's demands

During the Gulf War, two British soldiers came under fire while they were on their own, deep in enemy territory. As they took cover in a shallow desert trench, one of them was hit and killed. The remaining soldier didn't want his friend's body to fall into the hands of the enemy and so, as darkness fell, he lifted him on to his shoulders and began to carry him back to safety. Though exhausted and in constant danger of ambush, he pushed himself until he reached his company some twenty-four hours later.

Such a story of great devotion and bravery captures our attention and admiration. Perhaps it's because we all hope that, under similar circumstances, we too would put the welfare of others before our own. Added to that, the inspiration of examples like this spur us on in our relationships and daily caring.

In the week that the story of the soldier surfaced, another hero caught the public's attention: a terrorist bomb was detonated on the crowded platform of a London station. As people fled screaming from the explosion, one man, a conductor, ran toward the source of the blast and began to administer first-aid to injured victims. He became the tabloid hero of the week.

LIVING EXAMPLES

While these selfless and heroic acts rightly capture attention and stir deep feelings, we are even more challenged by those people whose lives demonstrate an ongoing commitment to others. These are the ones who have become living examples of the demanding love of God; the love which is best defined in the words of Jesus, 'So in everything, do to others what you would have them do to you...' (Matthew 7:12).

Who comes to mind when you think of someone whose life is a demonstration of love? If this question were the subject of a poll, then Mother Teresa would probably get more votes than any other person in the world. This frail woman has gained the respect of millions through her devotion to the poor of Calcutta. And through her example countless young people have volunteered for community service activities or overseas relief projects.

I was recently moved to tears by another example of love and devotion. A very successful theologian and college president retired at the height of his successful career so he could take care of his wife, a victim of Alzheimer's desease. Over the previous ten years, she had gradually lost her memory, control of her body and most of the abilities and characteristics that made her the woman her husband loved. At the time of the husband's decision to retire, she hadn't recognised him or their children for more than a year. Brain deterioration has left her requiring

the
love
story

more intensive care than a new-born baby.

Friends and colleagues suggested he should find a good institution for his wife, but he patiently explained, 'This lovely woman gave me the best years of her life. How could I abandon her now? Besides, when I married her, I made a vow, 'For better, for worse; for richer, for poorer; in sickness and in health - till death us do part.' That was not a casual remark, I meant it. The least I can do is stand by her in our old age.'

I was inspired by that story because there is a part of me that knows I was created to live a life of love, and that love is best expressed when it requires sacrifice. Love is demanding.

SACRIFICIAL PATH

Not many of us are called to work with the poor people of Calcutta. Few of us are likely to have to care for a husband or wife with Alzheimer's. But we know we should be more like these people who love so deeply and sacrificially.

I hope these few examples have provoked you to ask: 'How can I be more like that?' You'll find some answers to this question in our next section of Bible readings.

John, who was referred to as 'the disciple whom Jesus loved' (John 13:23), has love as the main theme of his Gospel as well as his letters. In them he clearly spells out its demands.

At any time in our lives we can take the path which will lead to a more loving and godly life. But that path is one of laying aside our own desires and plans and inviting God to take control. When we allow him to do this he will introduce circumstances and people which will test, shape and develop within us the qualities of love.

Of course, John wasn't the only New Testament writer to spell out the meaning of love. Paul penned a passage which goes very well with what John has to say on the subject. 1 Corinthians 13 explains what love is - and what it is not.

Love is: patient, kind, rejoices with truth, always protects, always trusts, always hopes, always perseveres.

Love does not: envy, boast, become proud or rude, seek self, become angry easily, keep a record of wrongs, or delight in evil.

This very practical and demanding list really hits home. But while I might draw some inspiration from someone like Mother Teresa and begin to think that I should try to do something for the poor of this world, God may well be wanting me to put aside those grandiose thoughts and be more patient with my children, or kinder to my wife. Love should always be most obvious in those relationships which are closest to us.

Before embarking upon our next group of readings, take a moment to ask for God's help to understand thoroughly what his word is saying. Ask for his help in applying it to every day life, so that you will make more progress on the path of love. With an honest and teachable heart and the help of the Holy Spirit, you could become one of those people who inspire others to live a more loving life.

Love's demands

Day 15
A NEW COMMANDMENT
1 John 2:7-17

On first sight, verses 7 and ·8 can seem somewhat confusing, because John says he is presenting an *old* commandment, and then claims it's a *new* one! So what exactly does he mean?

The commandment talked about is the commandment to love one another. This is nothing new, in the sense that people at all times and in all places have understood something of who God is (Romans 1:18-25) and his desire that we should love one another.

It is a new commandment though, in the sense that Jesus shed so much new light on the meaning of love. His whole life, teaching and death bring added depth to its meaning. So in that sense, it's truly new.

Verses 15 to 17 mention the danger of loving 'the world'. Christians have often found it difficult to interpret exactly what the Bible means by 'the world'. As a result, some have become very legalistic in their efforts to separate themselves from it. However, we are given a good explanation of what is meant (v 16). If we find ourselves craving the things we see, or if we have placed our security in what we have, then we are loving the world. Thank God that, in him, we can be free from such empty and enslaving pursuits.

Day 16
HOLD ON TO TRUTH
1 John 2:18-29

These verses repeat and emphasise some of the teaching John and the other disciples received from Jesus on the night of the last supper. Check the many similarities between this passage and the words of Jesus (John chapters 13-17). Especially notice the stark warnings about the spirit of antichrist which seeks to deceive us.

Even though we should take these warnings seriously, there is no reason to be afraid. If we hold on to the truth, the enemy will be unable to lead us astray. To help us work this through, John puts forward three suggestions:

● *Be careful* of anyone who denies that Jesus Christ is the Son of God. This is the central truth of the Christian message, and one which every cult ends up denying.

● *Hold on* to the anointing of the Spirit of God. If we seek to be sensitive to the Holy Spirit, we will know when his anointing has begun to lift. That should always be a danger signal to us.

● *Be committed* to righteous living (v 29).

the
love
story

Prayer starter:
Ask God to help you be attentive to these three principles, and be able to 'hold fast to the truth in love'.

Day 17
BECOME LIKE JESUS
1 John 3:1-10

the love story

It's incredible, but true: we *can* be like Jesus! When we commit ourselves to walk down the demanding path of love, we start a process of becoming more and more like him.

Have you ever met an elderly person who, having pursued a long life of love and obedience to Jesus, positively glows with love for Jesus? That is certainly how I'd like to be as I grow older.

However, if we want to become more godly and Christ-like, there is a price to be paid. Verse 6 reminds us that, 'No one who lives in him keeps on sinning.' If we want to be like Jesus, then we *must* declare a life-long war against sin. It's no good just accepting sinful behaviour as an unavoidable part of life. When we fall into that trap, we begin to be *less* like Jesus and *more* bound to bad habits, unloving attitudes and other kinds of sin.

Some misinterpretations of the Bible have implied that Christians can go on living sinful lives and that God will turn a blind eye and continue to accept them as righteous. This letter of John repeatedly makes it very clear that to keep on sinning wilfully means we are *not* God's children (v 10).

Prayer starter:
Help me, Lord, to resist the sins and temptations that I try to ignore. Please give me the power to overcome...

Day 18
LOVE ONE ANOTHER
1 John 3:11-18

'Love's demands' is certainly the right title for this series of readings. It's obvious the Christian life is not for the half-hearted. If we want to be Christ-like (*the meaning of 'Christian'*), then we must give ourselves to him without reservation, remembering that we are required to love others. And love them even to the point of being willing to lay down our lives for them. The demand for this depth of love certainly makes most of the difficulties, strains and differences we experience with our Christian family seem very petty. It's also quite obvious that what we might look on as 'normal' difficulties in those relationships, are unacceptable to God.

How do we know if we are loving others in the way God wants?

Well, we shouldn't evaluate ourselves by how we relate to those we find it easy to love. It's best to think about how we are expressing love to those we wouldn't normally get on with.

Prayer starter:
Action and sincerity are the tests of love. 'Let us not love with words or tongue but with actions and in truth.'

Talk to God about any action you need to be taking, but ask him to give you the gift of his love and compassion.

Love's demands

Day 19
LISTEN TO GOD
1 John 3:19-24

How would you like to be completely confident that you could stand before God without fear or condemnation? Would you like to be consistently full of the Holy Spirit? Or, perhaps have all your prayers answered, knowing that God would grant whatever you asked?

Well, according to today's Bible verses, these are the very things God wants for us, and he has shown *how* we can have them. Three conditions are highlighted. Once again, they are things which John, the disciple, heard from Jesus.

● *Love one another.* If we have loved others 'with actions and in truth', then we will not be condemned by our own hearts as we stand before Father God.

● *Believe in Jesus Christ.* This means being fully convinced that Jesus *was* and *is* the Son of God, and that everything he said about himself is true. This is the essential foundation for all faith and therefore, a necessity for our prayers to be answered.

● *Obey his commands.* And, as a result 'live in him'. Close fellowship with Jesus is the outcome of listening, talking and carefully doing all he has told us to do. Just as he was able to say he had done all his Father gave him to do (John 15:10), so must we.

Day 20
LIVE IN THE SPIRIT
1 John 4:1-6

These past few years seem to have brought a huge growth in spiritual activity. Young people are often involved in a variety of spiritual experiences, ranging from obvious occult practices through to some of the fantasy computer games with overtones of evil spirits. To further complicate matters, various inter-faith initiatives are being promoted by voices in high places. They seem to be saying that Jesus Christ and Christianity present just *one* of many ways to the same God.

With all of these different people claiming that their experiences and philosophies are from God, we need some way to judge what is true and what is deceitful. John emphasises the importance of testing all these things *and* spells out how to go about it:

● If any spirit or idea or experience acknowledges that Jesus is the Christ, the Son of God, then it is from God (v 2).

● If it denies anything about the divine nature of Jesus, his death or his resurrection, then it is not from God – no matter how good it might look (v 3).

For action:
When we are confused by the claims and teaching of others, it helps to talk with other Christians and to pray together.

the
love
story

That bit more...

The Bible readings in this section have made it very clear that God expects us to love *all* other people, especially Christians.

RELATIONSHIPS This commandment to love others was not just theory to the apostles who wrote about it. Do you remember how, in the book of *Acts,* Paul was harassed and persecuted by the Jews in most of the towns and cities he visited? Now look up Romans 9:3. God had so worked in Paul's heart and mind that he had a deep and sacrificial love – even for those who had made life so hard for him. The same Holy Spirit who gave Paul such a determined love, will also help you to love others.

FORGIVENESS If God has convicted you of any relationships which are not right, don't hesitate to ask him for forgiveness. Then ask him to give you the wisdom to know how to restore that relationship. It may be that the other person will not respond but, even so, God wants you to work at loving everyone.

WHAT LOVE IS You can make it easier for others to love you too. Have another look at 1 Corinthians 13 where Paul explains what love is and what it isn't. With the help of the Holy Spirit, each one of us can continue to grow in these very practical ways of being more loving and easier to love.

extra

Day 21
LOVE MADE PERFECT
1 John 4:7-21

The many challenges and demands in these verses leave no doubt at all that we were created to be loved by God and to love him and others in return. Because we sometimes fail to love as we should, we may feel discouraged, condemned and guilty. That is why John says: 'And so we know and rely on the love God has for us' (v 16).

We can be free from the fear of God's wrath because we know he loves us so much. Even though we have not perfectly loved others, we are so loved by God that we do not have to fear how he might treat us. On the other hand, we can rely on God's love within us to help us love in a measure beyond our own ability. The love of God living in us is capable of loving when we are not.

Everyone experiences times when certain people or circumstances tend to bring out the worst. Can you think of specific situations in which your reactions and behaviour have not been loving? Perhaps you would even feel that in certain situations it would be impossible for you to be loving. Well, that's when we get a chance to prove the truth of scripture and the fact that God's Spirit lives within us.

Prayer starter:
Call on God in faith. Remember his love can rise up within us and make love for the unlovable possible.

Love's demands

Available to all

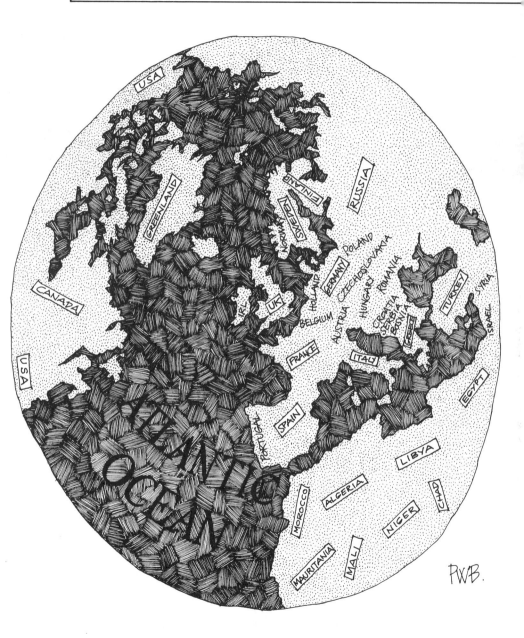

Wherever we live, whatever our nationality, God's love is available to us. It's effect on our lives is so powerful that the world can be turned upside down as we go forward in the name of Jesus.

Recently, a friend of mine visited for a few hours so we could discuss and pray about some plans for his ministry. During our time together, he recounted the remarkable things God had been doing in his life. When I said goodbye, I was left with a renewed hunger for God and a sense of excited anticipation about what God may want to do in my life and in the lives of Christians all over this land.

the love story

My friend told me how he had recently been in Korea, participating in a worship conference of some 80,000 people. Many of the things he experienced there were life-changing. But what had really impressed him was the way so many of the people he'd just met loved to pray.

In some inexplicable way, that love for prayer had 'rubbed off' on him.

He returned home with a deep desire to get closer to God in prayer. He told me of how he had since woken up in the middle of the night, with a great desire to pray. Sometimes this resulted in his getting dressed and going for a prayer-walk in a nearby park.

OVERWHELMING AND AWESOME

He tried to describe how, on one of those occasions, he'd felt overwhelmed with the presence of God as Judge, and was gripped by an awesome fear. That fear was relieved by a vision of the cross. It showed him that everything was forgiven and he was totally acceptable before God in spite of all his short-comings. Then the Holy Spirit began to pour his love into my friend. All this was such an overwhelming and intense experience that it left a permanent mark on him. He has a sense of closer fellowship with God and a deeper commitment to live a life of simple obedience to God's word. These are qualities we would all like to know more of. The question is, are they available to *every* Christian or only reserved for a special few?

FOR YOU AND ME

Both the Bible and church history indicate that the power of God's love is available to us all. Our next series of readings begins with one of Paul's wonderful prayers. In it, he asks God to give the Christians in Ephesus this same kind of supernatural revelation of the love of God. Paul says: 'And I pray that you, being rooted and established in love, may have power, together with all the saints, to grasp how wide and long and high and deep is the love of Christ, and to know this love that surpasses knowledge – that you may be filled to the measure of all the fullness of God' (Ephesians 3:17-19).

That sounds like a good description of what my friend experienced. And if Paul could pray for the early Christians to receive such a powerful revelation, then it's safe to assume that God would be willing to give the same blessing to us today.

There is ample evidence that he has

vailable to all

consistently poured out this power of love throughout the history of the church. For wherever women or men have sought him fervently, they have experienced an intense, close presence of God himself.

D L Moody, the great evangelist, is just one example. He experienced a 'baptism of love', and became a man of such great energy and natural enthusiasm, that he proved unstoppable once he had discovered the joy of leading people to Christ. In Chicago, where his ministry began, he became known as 'Crazy Moody', because his zeal and apparent lack of wisdom often resulted in eccentric behaviour.

Everywhere he went Moody confronted people, often beginning a conversation with a blunt question, such as, 'Are you a Christian yet, sir?' Or, 'What have you done for Christ today?' Then, as often as not, he would rush on to confront someone else.

In 1871, the Great Chicago Fire destroyed Moody's home and the mission school he had built. At the same time as this hit him, he was going through a personal crisis of spiritual dryness. Later that same year, while in New York, everything came to a head.

In his outstanding biography, *Moody without Sankey,* John Pollock recounts how this great evangelist craved spiritual power: 'He began to pace New York's streets at night, wrestling, panting for a Pentecost.' A short time after, as he walked down one of the busiest streets, he fully surrendered to God and declared his willingness to go wherever God would lead him. At that moment, '... an overpowering sense of the presence of God flooded his soul.

'God Almighty seemed to come very near. I felt I must be alone.' He hurried to the house of a friend nearby, sent up his card, and brushed aside an invitation for a meal. 'I want to be alone,' he said. Let me have a room where I can lock myself in.'

Moody's own description of that day was: 'I can only say that God revealed himself to me, and I had such an experience of his love that I had to ask him to stay his hand.'

From then on, he was a changed man. All his natural strength and enthusiasm was tempered by gentleness and compassion. He went on to reach millions of people in Europe and North America with the Good News of Jesus Christ.

Though few of us are likely to change a generation to the extent Moody did, all of us are called to fellowship with God and need more of his gracious love in our lives. As you read about the power of love from the book of *Ephesians,* allow God to apply it to your life so that you will be drawn closer to him. Then the power of his love will shine more brightly through you into the lives of others.

the
love
story

Day 22
FIRM FOUNDATIONS
Ephesians 3:14-21

the
love
story

Paul's great prayer, which he prayed for all the Christians at Ephesus, is a good prayer for us to use for ourselves and others.

It seems that, in both the history of the church and in church life today, some people make a much greater impact for God than others. *Why*? Are they more energetic, more committed?

As we read the biographies of great Christians, or as we listen to the experiences of those who are being very fruitful for God today, they seem to have at least one thing in common – most can recount a time when they had a deep revelation of the love of God. In other words, they experienced an answer to this prayer of Paul's, and began to have the power to 'grasp how wide and long and high and deep is the love of Christ...'

Many Christians have described this kind of 'baptism in love' as a turning-point, a time when God laid firm foundations of love in their lives.

For action:
Why not get together with one or two Christians and share your experiences of any 'turning-points' in your lives?

Pray together, asking for a greater experience of God's love.

Day 23
ROCK SOLID IN CHRIST
Ephesians 4:1-16

Paul, having prayed that individual Christians might have a revelation of God's love, now goes on to talk about how to work out that love with other Christians.

He presents that wonderful image of the church as a body, with every part working in complete harmony and interdependence with the other parts. However, this image of unity is dependent upon the love of God in each individual Christian.

Look again at the progression in this letter: first, Paul prays that each believer might receive a deeper revelation of the love of God (Day 22); next, he urges them to express this love to one another in humility, gentleness, patience and forbearance (v 2); then he goes on to write about a mature body of believers, being built up in love and power (vs 7-16).

From this we can see clearly that God expects *every* Christian to express their commitment to Christ in the context of a church. If our love for Jesus is not demonstrated by a loving unity with other believers, then that love falls short. But when we do love God and commit ourselves whole heartedly to loving others in a body of believers, then the love of Jesus Christ will be at work in that body. As a result, each member can become increasingly mature and rock solid in the love of Christ.

Available to all

Day 24
CHANGED LIVES
Ephesians 4:17-32

The proof of the love of God in you and me is the power we have to live a changed life. Paul describes it as putting off the old and putting on the new (vs 22-24). Romans 6 uses similar terminology, but Paul adds that our old self 'was crucified' with Jesus (6:6).

The 'old self' he is referring to consists of all wrong desires and tendencies toward bad attitudes, which are sometimes very strong and demanding. At those times, our vulnerability means we might easily give in to the 'old self' and land up with a guilty conscience. Or, on the other hand, we might fight against the temptation while still feeling condemned that we should even have such wrong attitudes or desires.

This is where the power of love comes in. God's love within us makes it possible to 'die to' or 'put off' those troublesome attitudes or desires. It may be painful, costly and demand a determined spirit but the power to live a changed life can be ours.

Think then pray:
We can count on the Holy Spirit to help us. He is always willing and available, for he wants us to 'put on the new self, created to be like God in true righteousness and holiness'. His power within us is what we need to live a changed life.

Day 25
IN CONTROL
Ephesians 5:1-20

Stop to think for a moment. These words were written over nineteen centuries ago, yet look at the list of common, but unacceptable, behaviour: sexual immorality, impurity, greed, obscenity, foolish talk, coarse joking, drunkenness and debauchery.

Such was the environment in which the believers at Ephesus lived. And our newspapers, television programmes, music, and other means of communication are all full of these things. The topics of conversation around us are also in the same vein. Human nature has not changed, and neither has God's message. In him, we *can* have sufficient power to be in control, even when faced with a flood of temptation.

We are warned to let no one deceive us (v 6). Don't listen to anyone who offers excuses for Christians to continue in unrighteous behaviour.

Prayer starter:
The Spirit has given us the power to be in control of our lives and to live them in purity. Take hold of his power and grow more like Jesus.

Father, you know the trouble I have with... I ask for your forgiveness and the power to overcome.

the
love
story

Day 26
MAKING MARRIAGE WORK
Ephesians 5:21-33

the
love
story

Marriages have always been under pressure. The reason is simple: for a marriage to be healthy, each partner must demonstrate an unselfish love. When people are too selfish to love sacrificially, they cannot make marriage work.

We are told to submit to one another. That word 'submit' means to voluntarily yield to another or to place oneself beneath another. Today, we hear a lot about each marriage partner protecting his or her rights within that marriage. But a good marriage begins with both partners being willing to give up their own rights and make a commitment to lovingly serve the other person.

In love, the wife is required to submit to her husband in *everything*.

For his part, the husband is required to *lay down his life* for his wife.

Which is the greater demand? They are the same. Each partner is required to put the other person first.

When a marriage breaks down it is often because one or both partners begins to concentrate on the obligations of the other person.

If a husband *demands* that his wife submit to him, he undermines their love.

When a wife *demands* more love and consideration, she may end up driving her husband away from her.

But when each *submits* to the other, love flourishes.

Day 27
FAMILY HARMONY
Ephesians 6:1-4

Whenever the Bible addresses any human relationship it is always very demanding because that is the nature of love. But it is also very fair, and today's Bible verses are a good example. They address *both* sides of the relationship and make quite equal demands. While, as children, we are required to honour and obey our parents, as parents we are commanded not to exasperate our children. The power of love should keep the peace. How does this work in your family?

Note a few important aspects of these family commandments: firstly, children are to obey whether or not they think their parents are right. This is often very hard, but God will honour those who obey him, especially when it is difficult. In addition, notice that there is no age limit on the commandment to obey and honour parents. While parents should not continue to issue orders to adult offspring, God expects us to go on honouring our parents.

Finally, fathers should note that God holds them responsible for child-rearing along with mothers. If it is literally impossible for a child to experience fatherly influence, as in the case of single mothers, then God will give grace to compensate, but he does not want fathers to abdicate their family responsibilities – no matter how busy they might be.

Available to all

Day 28
STANDING UP TO THE ENEMY
Ephesians 6:10-20

The power of God's love is sufficient protection against any spiritual attacks. In our reading, the picture is one of a well-protected Christian winning battles against the kingdom of darkness through prayer.

The context of this 'spiritual warfare' passage is important: it comes after all the commands and encouragements to live in loving relationships in the church and in the family. Once we have dealt with the old self and put on the new, we are ready to be victorious over all the spiritual forces of evil.

Until now, Paul has been urging us to lay hold of God's power in order to love others and overcome our tendency to sin. But the battle is actually bigger than that. We are not just overcoming a wayward nature and the awkwardness of other people; we are in a fight against supernatural powers.

However, God has given us supernatural protection and the spiritual weapons we need for victory, so there is no reason to be afraid of our adversary. It's Satan and his dark kingdom who have every reason to fear.

Prayer starter:
Father, I want to live in the power of your love, to plunder Satan's kingdom, by bringing more and more people out of darkness and into your light.

Change the world

We are engaged in a great battle, but we have the power to stand and be victorious. That's been the consistent theme of this last section's readings.

Have you ever thought you would like to accomplish something significant in this world? Have you wondered how, as a Christian, you can make a bigger impact for God? Well, there is a way to become a world-changer.

BATTLE ON! Notice the way the battle is identified in *Ephesians:* Make a note of verses which tell us that much of the battle takes place within us and is against wrong desires and attitudes. The battle is also waged in our relationships, especially in families and church.

VICTORY Take hold of the power of God's love which is available to you. With the Holy Spirit bringing the love of Jesus into your life you can have victory within, as well as the power to love others.

TRUST Rely on God's promise of protection and power in facing Satan and his kingdom. As we learn to live in this power of love, God 'is able to do immeasurably more than all we ask or imagine, according to his power that is at work within us' (Ephesians 3:20). That's the power of love!

extra

WHAT NEXT!

You've finished this book. What are you going to do about Bible reading now? Well, for a start, there are four other *Growing with Jesus* books. If you have already worked through all of those, Scripture Union offers a choice of three different styles of notes for adults. One of them should suit you!

You may order GWJ books and Scripture Union notes from
- your local Christian bookshop ● your Scripture Union church representative
- by post from Scripture Union Mail order.

SU ADULT BIBLE READING NOTES

DAILY BREAD Practical help from the Bible for everyday Christian living. £1.60 quarterly

ALIVE TO GOD Bible exploration for living by the Spirit. £1.60 quarterly

DAILY NOTES An in-depth reflection for more experienced Bible readers. £1.60 quarterly

GROWING WITH JESUS SERIES

the ME problem by Rob Warner

the LOVE story by Lynn Green

the POWER dimension by Michael Cole

the GOD slot by Philip Mohabir

the PRAYER principle by Jim Graham

- -

ORDER FORM

To: Scripture Union Mail Order, 9-11 Clothier Road, Bristol BS4 5RL
Tel: (0272) 719709 24 hr order line Fax: (0272) 711472

GWJ Books	Total		Quantity	Price
Me problem (£2.25*)	_____	Daily Bread (£9.20*) _____		
Love Story (£2.25*)	_____	Daily Notes (£9.20*) _____		
Power dimension (£2.25*)	_____	Alive to God (£9.20*) _____		
God slot (£2.25*)	_____	**Total**		
Prayer principle (£2.25*)	_____			

*Including UK postage and packing.   (*Payment with order please*)

Please send me one year's supply of the above notes starting

☐ **January**   ☐ **April**   ☐ **July**   ☐ **October** (*please tick one*)

Overseas rates Europe +£1.50 per subscription. Outside Europe +£3.00 per subscription.
PLEASE USE BLOCK CAPITALS

Name _____

Address _____

_____ Postcode _____

I enclose CHEQUE/POSTAL ORDER amount £ _____

Please debit my ACCESS/BARCLAYCARD amount £ _____

| | | | | | | | | | | | | | | | | | Expiry date | | | | |

In **Australia**, write for subscription details to: Scripture Union, 241 Flinders Lane, Melbourne, Vic 3000.
In **USA**, write for subscription details to: Scripture Union, 7000 Ludlow Street, Upper Darby, PA 19082.
In **Canada**, write for subscription details to: Scripture Union, 1885 Clements Road, Unit 226, Pickering, Ontario, L1W 3V4. In **South Africa**, write for subscription details to: Scripture Union, Millard House, 83 Camp Ground Road, Rondebosch 7700.

GWJ94